DISCARD

CHECKERBOARD HOW-TO LIBRARY

COOL ART

COOL SCULPTURE

THE ART OF CREATIVITY
FOR KIDS!

ANDERS HANSON

ABDO
Publishing Company

CONTENTS

Published by ABDO Publishing Company, 8000 West 78th Street, Edina, Minnesota 55439.

Copyright © 2009 by Abdo Consulting Group, Inc. International copyrights reserved in all countries.

No part of this book may be reproduced in any form without written permission from the publisher. Checkerboard Library™ is a trademark and logo of ABDO Publishing Company.

Printed in the United States.

Editor: Pam Price

Series Concept: Nancy Tuminelly

Cover and Interior Design: Anders Hanson, Mighty Media

Photo Credits: Anders Hanson, Shutterstock, Colleen Dolphin, Matthias Kabel (Venus of Willendorf, p. 4)

Play-Doh® is a registered trademark of Hasbro, Inc.

Library of Congress Cataloging-in-Publication Data

Hanson, Anders, 1980-

Cool sculpture : the art of creativity for kids / Anders Hanson.
     p. cm. -- (Cool art)

Includes index.

ISBN 978-1-60453-144-2

1. Sculpture--Technique--Juvenile literature. I. Title.

NB1170.H28 2008

731.4--dc22

2008022324

Get the Picture!

When a step number in an activity has a colored circle around it, look for the picture that goes with it. The picture's border will be the same color as the circle.

2 ·············>

THE ART OF creativity

You Are Creative

Being creative is all about using your imagination to make new things. Coming up with new ideas and bringing them to life is part of being human. Everybody is creative! Creative thinking takes time and practice. But that's okay, because being creative is a lot of fun!

Calling All Artists

Maybe you believe that you aren't good at art. Maybe you have some skills that you want to improve. The purpose of this book is to help you develop your visual creativity. Remember that your artistic skills improve every time you make art. The activities in this book can help you become the creative artist you want to be!

Creativity Tips

- Stay positive.
- There is no wrong way to be creative.
- Allow yourself to make mistakes.
- Tracing isn't cheating.
- Practice, practice, practice.
- Be patient.
- Have fun!

SCULPTURE IS COOL!

Every block of stone has a statue inside it and it is the task of the sculptor to discover it.
—Michelangelo

PIETÀ (1499)
— MICHELANGELO

What Is Sculpture?

Sculpture is three-dimensional art. Unlike flat art, such as paintings or drawings, sculptures look different from different angles. Sculpture can represent something real, or it can come from the artist's imagination. Sculptures can be as small or as large as the artist wants. A person who creates sculpture is called a sculptor.

Stone, metal, clay, and wood are commonly used to make sculptures. But a sculpture can be made from almost anything. Artists use different **techniques** to create sculptures. Most sculpting techniques can be grouped into four main processes. They are carving, modeling, casting, and assembling.

Prehistoric Sculpture

In prehistoric times, hunters skillfully carved tools out of stone and wood. Later, they discovered that they could also use these carving skills to create art. One of the oldest known pieces of art is a small, stone statue of a pregnant woman. It's called the Venus of Willendorf. It's about 25,000 years old!

THE VENUS OF WILLENDORF

Be a Sculptor!

Learning to sculpt is easy and fun! It's easy because all you need to start is a piece of clay. It's fun because you can do anything that your imagination comes up with!

If you are not satisfied with your first sculptures, remember this. Great artists are not always satisfied with their work. Part of what makes them great is that they are always trying to get better. You don't need to be good at art now to become a great artist. You just need the desire to learn and become better!

***THE THINKER* (1880) — AUGUSTE RODIN**

Don't Be a Judge!

When discussing a work of art, avoid using the words listed below. They offer judgments without saying much about the character of the work. Instead, look at how the artist used composition and techniques. Try to understand what the artist was trying to achieve. See pages 8 through 13 to read about these elements.

- good
- bad
- right
- wrong
- silly
- stupid

Have Patience

Be patient with yourself. Changes won't happen overnight. When you make a sculpture that you don't like, don't throw it out. Save it so you can look back later and see how much you've improved! Have **confidence** in yourself. You can do anything you set your mind to!

TOOLS OF THE TRADE

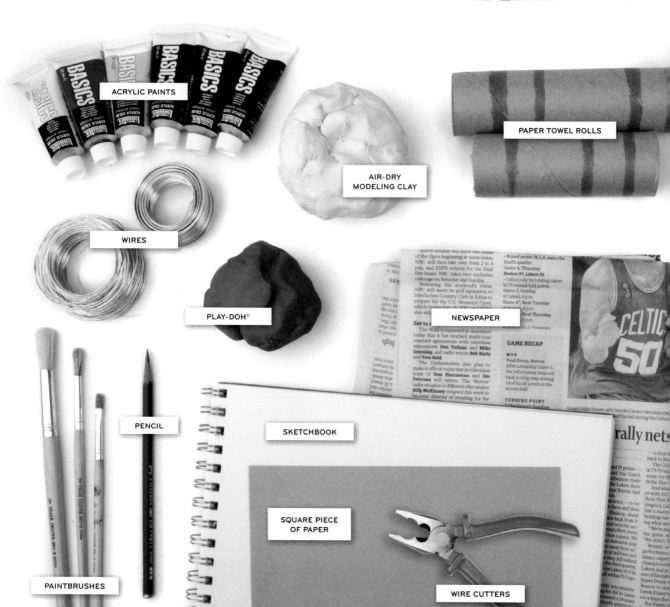

ACRYLIC PAINTS

AIR-DRY MODELING CLAY

PAPER TOWEL ROLLS

WIRES

PLAY-DOH®

NEWSPAPER

PENCIL

SKETCHBOOK

SQUARE PIECE OF PAPER

PAINTBRUSHES

WIRE CUTTERS

Each activity in this book has a list of the tools and materials you will need. When you come across a tool you don't know, turn back to these pages. You can find most of these items at your local art store.

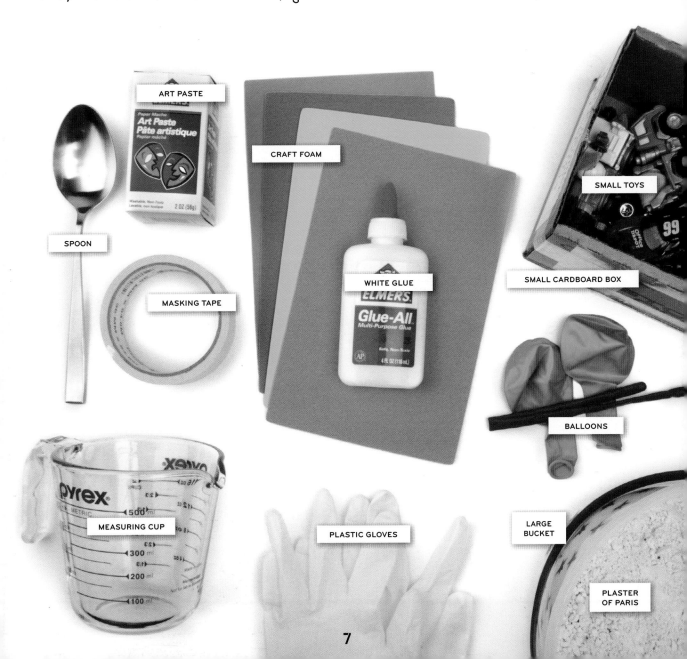

ART PASTE

CRAFT FOAM

SMALL TOYS

SPOON

WHITE GLUE

SMALL CARDBOARD BOX

MASKING TAPE

BALLOONS

MEASURING CUP

PLASTIC GLOVES

LARGE BUCKET

PLASTER OF PARIS

Basic Elements

These are the elements that make up sculptures. Sculptures can be described by these key **concepts**.

Line

A line has length but very little width or depth. It is almost one-dimensional. Wires and strings are examples of lines. Lines can be straight or curved.

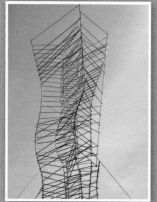

Plane

A plane has length and width but not much depth. It is essentially two-dimensional. A piece of paper is an example of a plane. Planes can be curved or straight. Some artists create sculpture using only planes.

CURVED PLANES

STRAIGHT PLANES

8

Volume

Volumes have length, width, and depth. They are three-dimensional. Volume is the most important element of sculpture because sculpture is three-dimensional.

There are many different kinds of volumes. A volume may be a simple **geometric** form, such as a pyramid, a cube, or a sphere. A volume can also have an **irregular** form, such as a person or a tree.

GEOMETRIC VOLUMES

IRREGULAR VOLUME

Texture

Texture is the quality, or feel, of a surface. The materials and methods used to create a sculpture determine its texture. Sculptures made of chiseled rock have a rough texture. Polished bronze sculptures have a smooth texture.

ROUGH TEXTURE

SMOOTH TEXTURE

Color

Sculptures are traditionally left unpainted. Most artists prefer the natural color of the material they sculpt with. Metal sculptures may change color over time because of chemical changes on the surface.

PAINTED

UNPAINTED

Composition

Bringing together the basic elements to make a work of art is called composition. The following ideas will help you create great compositions!

Movement

Sculptures can suggest motion without actually moving. In figurative sculpture, this is done by positioning the body in an action pose. Some sculptures, such as mobiles, actually move. These are called **kinetic art**.

SUGGESTED MOVEMENT

KINETIC SCULPTURE

Balance

In sculpture, balance is linked to symmetry. If a sculpture is symmetrical, it looks balanced. Asymmetrical sculptures often look like they might fall over. They are unbalanced.

BALANCED

UNBALANCED

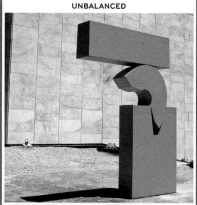

Space

The space that a sculpture takes up is called positive space. The space around a sculpture is called negative space. When these spaces work well together, the sculpture is more interesting.

SCULPTURE

POSITIVE SPACE

NEGATIVE SPACE

Scale

Sculptures can be huge or tiny. The scale of a sculpture affects how we relate to it. Sculptures that are larger than a person often inspire a sense of awe.

LARGE SCALE

SMALL SCALE

Michelangelo's David

Michelangelo's famous sculpture of David is 17 feet (5.2 m) tall. That's about three times the height of an average man. Imagine that Michelangelo had made David just 4 feet (1.2 m) tall. Instead of looking up to the sculpture, people would look down at it. A smaller version of David would not seem as mighty or as heroic.

Techniques

These are the four major types of **techniques** used to create sculpture.

Modeling

Modeling is the process of building up soft material to create a sculpture. Clay and wax are popular modeling materials. In modeling, a sculptor continually adds bits of material to create the basic form. Using bare hands or tools, the sculptor then shapes the material until the sculpture is finished.

Carving

Carving is the process of removing material to create a sculpture. The sculptor starts with a solid block of hard material. He or she uses tools to cut away bits and pieces until the desired form is achieved. Stone and wood are common carving materials.

Casting

Casting is the method of forming liquid material into a solid sculpture. Molten metal, concrete, and plaster are liquids commonly used in casting.

First the artist makes a mold of a sculpture. The hollow space inside the mold is the final shape of the sculpture. Then the sculptor pours liquid into the mold. The liquid fills the mold and assumes the shape of the hollow space. It is allowed to cool or dry until the liquid becomes a solid. The mold is then removed, revealing the sculpture.

CONCRETE

METAL

PLASTER

Assembling

Assembling is the process of joining solid objects to form a sculpture. Wood and metal are popular materials for assembling. But the objects can be made of almost any material. The way they are joined depends on the type and weight of the material. Metal objects can be **welded** together. Wood objects are often joined with glue.

WIRE FRAME

Create and pose this flexible figure!

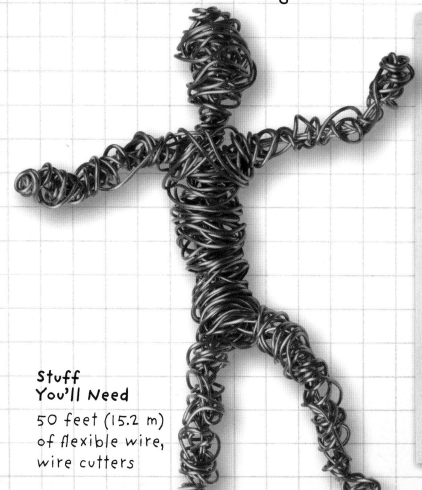

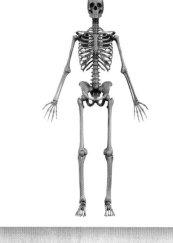

The Skeleton

A skeleton determines how tall or short a person is. It also affects the size of the head and the length of the arms and legs. Study the proportions of the skeleton above to make a more realistic wire figure.

Stuff You'll Need

50 feet (15.2 m) of flexible wire, wire cutters

1. Make a stick figure out of wire. Begin by bending one end of the wire to form a loop. This will be the figure's head.

2. Make the arms from the same piece of wire. Try to make them the same length. Leave a little wire between the head and the arms for the neck.

3. Now form the body and the legs. The body should be slightly shorter than the arms. Bend the wire below the body to make the legs. Note that the legs are a little longer than the arms.

4. Wrap the loose end of the wire around the area where the body meets the legs. Then wrap it around the shoulder area a few times. This completes the stick figure. But don't cut the wire yet!

5. Wrap some of the loose wire around the body. Don't wrap it too tightly though.

6. Continue wrapping the wire around the figure's body, arms, head, and legs until you're happy with the figure's shape. Cut the wire and tuck the end into the body.

7. Pose the figure in any position you choose.

SUPERHERO

Create a new superhero from your imagination!

Muscle System

The shape of a body is influenced by muscles. Use the illustration below to see where the muscles go.

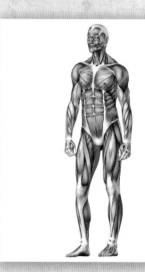

Stuff You'll Need

Wire figure, air-dry modeling clay, acrylic paints, small paintbrush

1   This project requires a completed wire-frame figure from the project on pages 14 and 15.

2   If you were a superhero, what kind of powers would you have? What would your superhero name be? Use your imagination to create your own hero. Your character can be male or female.

3   What kind of pose do you want your superhero to have? Bend the wire figure to match that pose.

4   Now begin covering the wire figure's body with clay. Don't worry about details such as fingers or facial features. Just try to get the basic form of the body.

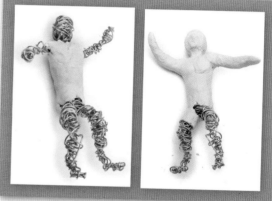

5   Continue to add bits of clay until all of the wire is covered.

6   Superheroes usually wear skintight suits. So, you can see big muscles in the chest, stomach, shoulders, thighs, buttocks, upper arms, and calves. To add muscles to your figure, place a slab of clay where the each muscle would be. Use your fingers to blend the edges of each slab into the body.

7   Allow the clay to completely dry. This can take several hours.

8   Paint your superhero however you like!

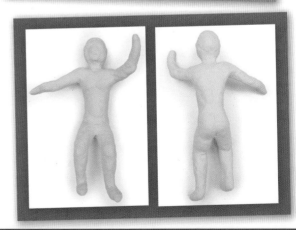

SWAN SONG

Make this traditional origami swan from just one piece of paper!

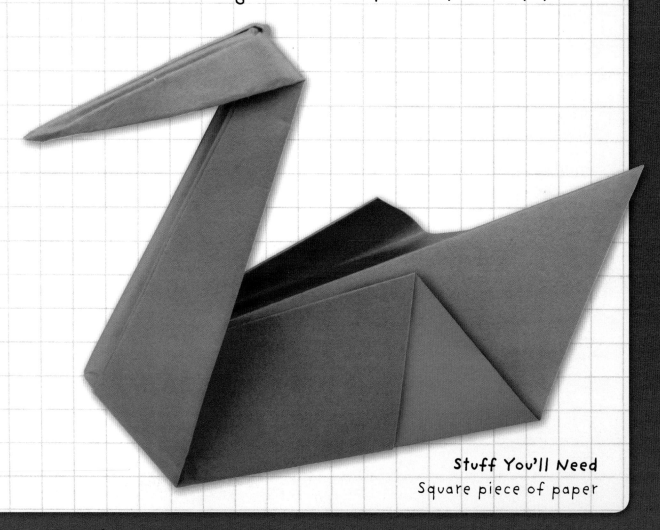

Stuff You'll Need
Square piece of paper

18

1. Rotate the paper square so the corners point straight up and down.

2. Fold the paper in half. Crease the folded edge. Unfold the paper.

3. Fold in the right edge so it aligns with the center crease. Repeat with the left edge. Your paper should look like a kite.

4. Flip the paper over.

5. Fold in the right and left edges so they meet at the center crease. Now the kite shape should have a sharp point at the bottom.

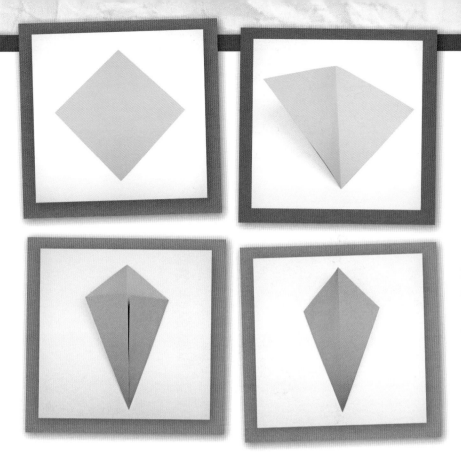

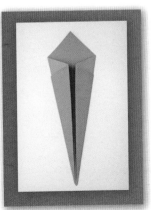

Origami

Origami is the art of paper folding. It became popular in Japan in the 1600s. Origami artists create sculptures from single pieces of paper. Most origami sculptures are made without cutting or gluing the paper.

6 Fold the sharp point up so that it's just below the top point. The bottom part of this fold will be the neck.

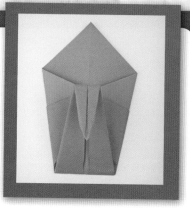

7 Fold the tip of the sharp point down to make the head.

8 Fold the shape in half lengthwise. Crease the fold.

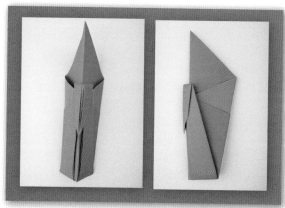

9 Gently pull the neck away from the body. When you're happy with its position, press the base of the neck flat.

10 Now pull the head away from the neck. Press the area between the head and the neck flat.

11 Separate the bottoms of the wings a little. This gives the swan a solid base to rest on.

20

CAST AWAY!

Make cool casts of your favorite toys!

Stuff You'll Need

Play-Doh®, small cardboard box, small toys, gloves,
plaster of Paris, measuring cup, large bucket, water, spoon

1 Collect small toys that you want to make a cast of. Choose one to start with.

2 Spread a layer of Play-Doh® a half-inch (1.3 cm) deep along the bottom of the small box. If your object is thicker, then the Play-Doh should be even deeper. Smooth the Play-Doh with your fingers.

3 Press the object firmly into the Play-Doh. Be careful not to mark the Play-Doh with your fingers or to push the object in too deep. Gently pull the object out of the Play-Doh. The object will leave an imprint.

4 If there is room, you can make impressions of other objects in the same mold. Repeat step three for any other objects you want to use.

5 Ask an adult to help you with the next few steps. Get out the plaster of Paris. Follow the instructions for safety on the package. Put on a pair of rubber gloves. Measure about two cups of plaster of Paris. Pour the plaster into a large, clean bucket.

6 Measure one cup of water. Add the water to the plaster a little bit at a time. Stir frequently. Stir the mixture until it is smooth.

7 Pour or spoon the wet plaster into the mold. Spread the plaster around evenly. You need to work quickly to finish before the plaster sets.

8 Allow to plaster to dry for one hour. Remove the cardboard box. Peel the Play-Doh away from the plaster cast and wash the cast.

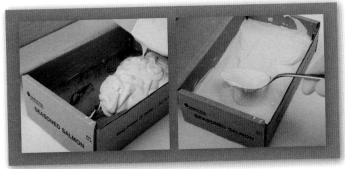

9 Dry the cast for 24 hours. Paint it however you like.

ART IN MOTION

Make a moving mobile!

The Mobile

A mobile is a system of hanging objects connected by wire. The objects are arranged so that the sculpture is balanced. Each object hangs from a single wire. This allows the objects to rotate in place. Because the objects can move, mobiles are considered **kinetic art**. Alexander Calder created the first mobile in 1931.

Stuff You'll Need

Craft foam, pencil, scissors, white glue, coil of thin wire, wire cutters

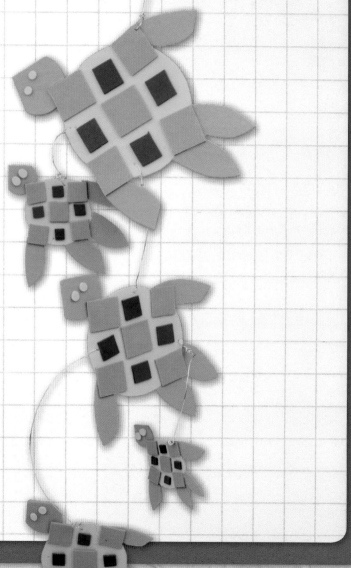

1 Think of an object to create using different-shaped foam pieces. It can be anything!

2 Once you have a plan, draw the shapes onto the foam. You can trace things to help make the shapes. Cut out the foam shapes.

3 Glue the foam pieces to each other. Make sure the sides without pencil lines are faceup.

4 Now make the same object, but this time make it a different size. Repeat this process until you have five objects that look alike but are different sizes. Set them aside until the glue dries.

5 After the glue is dry, arrange the objects on the table as you would like them to hang. Think about weight and balance.

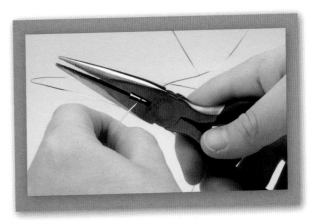

6 When you have the objects placed where you want them, cut a piece of wire that is about 6 to 7 inches (15.2 to 17.8 cm) long. Have an adult help you cut the wire.

7 Poke the wire through the edge of the first foam object. Slide through about 1.5 inches (3.8 cm) of the wire. Loop the wire and twist it to close the loop.

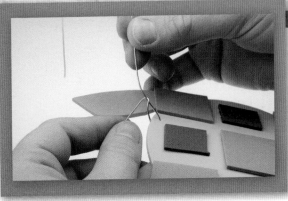

8 Curve the remaining wire.

9 Poke the end of the wire through the next object that will hang from it. Loop the wire and twist it closed. Repeat steps 6 through 9 until all of the objects are joined by wires.

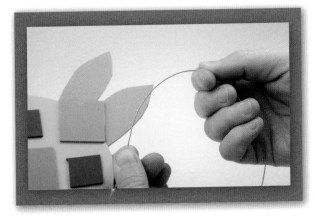

10 When all of the objects are connected, cut a piece of wire that is about 10 inches (25.4 cm) long. Poke it through the top object. Loop the wire and twist it closed. Straighten the remaining wire and create a large loop at the other end. Twist the wire to close the loop. Now you can hang the mobile!

MONSTER MANIA

Scare up some papier-mâché sculpture!

Stuff You'll Need
Sketchbook,
pencil, balloons,
newspaper,
paper towel rolls,
masking tape,
art paste, water,
acrylic paint,
paintbrushes

1. What do you want your monster to look like? Using your imagination, draw different monster characters. Keep in mind the materials you'll be using to create them, such as paper towel rolls for arms and legs. Choose the one you like best to make into a three-dimensional sculpture.

2. Now, using a balloon, newspaper, and paper towel rolls, start building your character. Use the masking tape to hold the pieces together. You can fold and crumple the newspaper into whatever shape you need. The finished shape should be strong enough to hold together while you apply the papier-mâché.

3. Next you'll need to make the papier-mâché paste. Mix the art paste with water according to the instructions on the package.

4. Tear strips of newspaper to dunk into the paste. Torn pieces work better than cut pieces.

5. Dip one piece of newspaper at a time. Make sure it is completely covered with paste. As you remove the newspaper strip, run it through your fingers to remove the excess paste. The strip should be **saturated** but not dripping.

6 Wrap the newspaper strips around the object. Layer the strips in different directions. Make sure to smooth the newspaper with your fingers. Keep overlapping the strips of newspaper until the object is entirely covered. Let it dry for 24 hours.

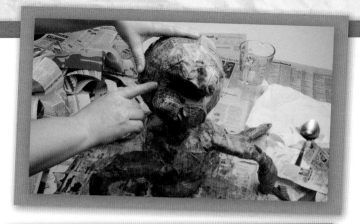

7 Add another layer of overlapping newspaper strips. Cover the entire object again. Let it dry for 24 hours.

8 Add one more layer of newspaper strips and let it dry again for 24 hours. You should have at least three layers covering your object.

9 Once your monster is completely dry, you can paint it and decorate it. Make sure to be careful when handling your monster. The arms and legs can be fragile.

10 If you want the monster to last a long time, have an adult help you apply varnish or acrylic sealing spray after the paint has dried.

what's next?

Taking Care of Your Sculptures

The best place to put a sculpture is where lots of people will see it. If you're not going to display your sculpture, make sure you store it properly. That way, you can show people how you got your start when you become famous!

A sculpture can be difficult to care for. Any part of a sculpture that sticks out is in danger of breaking. One solution is to store the sculpture in a box. Find a cardboard box that's a little larger than the sculpture. Place the sculpture inside and fill the box with foam peanuts or bubble wrap.

Try Something New!

The activities in this book are just a few examples of fun sculpture projects you can do. Once you've completed them all, try some of the projects again with different materials or subjects. Then make up some projects of your own!

Start Seeing Sculpture!

One of the best ways to learn about sculpture is to see it in person! A photo of a sculpture can show only one side of it. Experiencing sculpture in three dimensions is much more interesting.

Visit a local museum or sculpture garden and bring a sketchbook. When you see an interesting sculpture, walk slowly around it. Study its form from different angles. Make a few quick sketches of the sculpture.

What was the sculptor trying to communicate? Think about how the artist used elements such as line, shape, volume, texture, and color. What materials and **techniques** do you think the artist used? Does the scale of the sculpture affect how you feel about it? Asking these kinds of questions can be helpful when trying to understand sculpture.

30

GLOSSARY

concept – an idea.

confidence – a feeling of faith in your own abilities.

geometric – made up of straight lines, circles, and other simple shapes.

irregular – lacking symmetry or evenness.

kinetic art – art that has parts that can be set in motion.

saturated – wet all the way through.

technique – a method or style in which something is done.

weld – to join metal parts by heating the metal until the parts melt together.

Web Sites

To learn more about cool art, visit ABDO Publishing Company on the World Wide Web at **www.abdopublishing.com**. Web sites about cool art are featured on our Book Links page. These links are routinely monitored and updated to provide the most current information available.

INDEX